YOU MIGHT NEED A THERAPIST IF...

John Carfi & Cliff Carle
with David W. Earle, LPC

Illustrations by Scott Sackett

Carle & Carfi Publishing
1931 S. Bentley Ave.
Los Angeles, CA 90025

Published with CreateSpace

YOU MIGHT NEED A THERAPIST IF...

Print book ISBN: 978-0-9834615-5-5
E-Book ISBN: 978-0-9834615-6-2

This book is intended for humor purposes only. Repeat any of the jokes herein at your own risk.

Cover Illustration and interior cartoons by Scott Sackett

Formatting by DeborahAnn Marshall

A special thanks to Jeff Foxworthy for the "You Might...If " format.

INTRODUCTION

Dear Reader,

Let's get something straight: Even though most of these jokes start out with "You", they're not actually about *you*. They're about *them*... all those other people: your cousins, uncles and aunts, siblings – sometimes parents – friends, acquaintances, neighbors, and a lot of those clueless cohorts at work. Many of these folks could really use some therapy, right? But you don't have to tell them that. It can be your little secret.

In fact, why not have fun matching up the jokes with people you know!

— John & Cliff

P.S. So, why did the writing team of Carfi & Carle pick up a free agent on this book? We'll let him explain..

INTRODUCTION #2

Laughter is natural, enjoyable, nonfattening, and has many health benefits. Laughter releases endorphins, which create a natural high, reducing stress and increasing relaxation. It even helps prevent the #1 killer: heart disease. Research has shown that one minute of *hearty laughter* can elevate your heart rate to the same level it reaches after 10 minutes on a rowing machine.

Cliff Carle was the editor on my self-help book *Love is Not Enough.* It included comic relief in the form of *You Might Be A Chaos Person If...* jokes. Afterwards, Cliff proposed the book you now hold in your hands. Since I have a large appreciation for absurdity while also being a licensed professional counselor, this combination appealed to John and Cliff's objectives and sense of humor. Hence, I became the team's late-round draft pick. But if you have any problems with this book, blame it on them.

Want to reduce your stress...laugh more. Want to be happy...choose a humorous attitude. Want to have better health...allow spontaneous humor. Would you rather spend 10 minutes on a rowing machine, or give yourself permission to have a hearty belly laugh?

— David W. Earle, LPC

YOU MIGHT NEED A THERAPIST IF ...

You'll beat the crap out of anyone who says you've got an attitude problem.

❖

You love your wife so much, you only have affairs with women who look like her.

❖

You're so wishy-washy, you proclaim to be an atheist, but pray you are wrong.

YOU MIGHT NEED A THERAPIST IF ...

You went on a diet that allows you to "cheat once in a while", then had sex with your neighbor's husband.

❖

You're so distrustful, if someone wants to borrow your pen, you ask for collateral.

❖

You heard that "two wrongs don't make a right" so you tried for three.

Reading is the best thing you do in bed.

❖

The only way you can have a good day
is if you know someone else is
having a bad one.

❖

Nothing gets you in the mood for love
like rejection.

When you were a kid, your imaginary
friend was the imaginary school bully.

❖

Every Sunday you put a $100 bill in the
collection plate;
after waving it high in the air
for everyone to see.

❖

You've been hiding in the attic ever since
you accidentally tore off that mattress tag.

YOU MIGHT NEED A THERAPIST IF …

You're so horny; you act suspicious at the airport
so Security will pat you down.

YOU MIGHT NEED A THERAPIST IF ...

Your motto is: "If at first you don't succeed — cry, cry again!"

❖

You're such a workaholic, you've forgotten your kids' names, ages, and how many you have.

❖

You masturbate then light up two cigarettes.

You just can't let go; you're still grieving over the death of that frog you dissected in high school biology class.

❖

You're so resentful, after the divorce you bulldozed your half of the house.

❖

Integrity to you is never admitting a mistake.

YOU MIGHT NEED A THERAPIST IF ...

To save time, you read yourself
your rights before leaving the house.

❖

You're such a high achiever, you studied
all night for your urine test.

❖

You think you are dying and someone
else's life flashes before your eyes.

YOU MIGHT NEED A THERAPIST IF ...

You are an egomaniac with
an inferiority complex.

❖

You're so overbooked, you've arranged to
have a stand-in cadaver
for your own funeral.

❖

When the going gets tough,
you wet your pants.

YOU MIGHT NEED A THERAPIST IF ...

Someone stole your identity, then turned themselves in rather than be you.

❖

You think you're just "accident prone" because you frequently find yourself hitting someone's fist with your face.

❖

When sitting at rest, your legs nervously bounce so fast, they look like hummingbird wings.

YOU MIGHT NEED A THERAPIST IF ...

Your motto is: "If the shoe fits... steal it!"

❖

You're so concerned with looking good,
you gave a homeless person a dollar,
then tipped him $5 bucks.

❖

For you, a picture is worth a *couple*
words: "This sucks!"

YOU MIGHT NEED A THERAPIST IF ...

You're such a smarty-pants, you believe
that if Einstein were alive,
he'd be your bitch.

❖

Rehab is a family tradition.

❖

You're so stoic, the last time you had a
good cry was when the doctor slapped
your butt in the delivery room.

You can resist anything, as long as anything doesn't include temptation.

❖

You couldn't care less that you're apathetic.

❖

Before sentencing, you point out all the procedural errors the judge made, then conclude with, "...and furthermore, you're an idiot!"

YOU MIGHT NEED A THERAPIST IF ...

You don't wear a watch because it
constantly reminds you that
time is running out!

❖

This is the hard-luck story you tell your
kids: "When I was your age,
my chauffeur wouldn't open
the limo door for me!"

❖

You watch Reality TV for the acting.

You're such a neat freak, you iron
your shoelaces.

❖

You bring a fishing pole on
a singles' cruise ship.

❖

Because none of your relatives will
come to your house, you think
they're a bunch of snobs —
and your 40 cats all agree.

You call in sick at least once a week -
even though you don't have a job.

Your favorite picnic spot is the cemetery.

❖

You get up in the middle of the night
and raid your neighbor's refrigerator.

❖

You're such a show-off, at the fast food
drive-thru you order in Pig Latin.

YOU MIGHT NEED A THERAPIST IF ...

You don't take "no" for an answer, because "maybe" will do.

❖

You're afraid of picking up hitchhikers because they might like you.

❖

Your motto is: "An apple a day keeps the doctor away... if you throw it hard enough."

YOU MIGHT NEED A THERAPIST IF ...

Your wardrobe has more black
than an undertaker's.

❖

You decide you need a new car with a
larger glove compartment to hold all your
unpaid parking tickets.

❖

You have a fear that the jet's going to
crash, but you're not on that one.

Your Attention Deficit Disorder is so bad,
sometimes you'll be in the middle
of a sentence and

❖

You're so transparent, ghosts
don't believe in you.

❖

You show up for your second date with
your stuff packed into a moving van.

YOU MIGHT NEED A THERAPIST IF ...

Your tough-love parenting style involves brass knuckles.

❖

You don't have a drinking problem, but you're so cheap, you go to AA meetings for the free coffee.

❖

The last time you were on time
— wait!
— you're never on time.

You vociferously proclaim you're not gay,
even though as an infant, you wanted
to be breast-fed by your dad.

❖

You put on work gloves when you pee.

❖

You dial 911 then hang up, because it's
the only way you can get someone
to call you back.

You deal with your bulimia by hanging out with really fat people.

❖

You can't breathe properly unless you're criticizing someone.

❖

Fear of flying? You're afraid of driving and even walking.

You're such a hypochondriac, you
converted your closet into a
walk-in medicine cabinet.

❖

You started a club for people
who hate belonging to clubs;
and now you're depressed because
you're the only member.

❖

You show up at work on "casual Fridays"
with no pants.

Your deep freezer has 30 quarts of ice cream, and one grandpa.

Your enemies list looks like the
New York City phone book.

❖

You're so polite, so as not to
disturb others, you talk
to yourself in sign language.

❖

You act as your own judge and jury,
and are proud of your
100% conviction rate.

You're so greedy, when you heard there's life after death, you bequeathed your entire fortune to yourself.

❖

You don't suffer from diarrhea, actually you kind of enjoy it.

❖

Two gorgeous women approach you in a bar and suggest a three-way; you respond: "Not tonight ladies, I'm here to get drunk."

*You always wear a tailored, 3-piece Armani suit to work,
even though the other lumberjacks tease you relentlessly.*

YOU MIGHT NEED A THERAPIST IF ...

You are so suicidal, you put on your left
blinker whenever you're turning right.

❖

When people treat you nice, you find
them annoying.

❖

You do not want to interrupt, so you
refrain from telling the warden about the
governor's last-minute pardon
of your execution.

Your idea of a compliment is: "You're much less ugly than my last girlfriend."

❖

You're so sensitive, while watching a movie on DVD, you cry during the "Piracy is Not a Victimless Crime" announcement.

❖

You're so oversexed, you have a premature orgasm when your grandma kisses you good-bye.

Whenever you're feeling down
and need cheering up, there's always
the obituary column.

❖

You hate parties because,
of course, they're all talking about you.

❖

You love parties because,
of course, they're all talking about you.

YOU MIGHT NEED A THERAPIST IF ...

In the background of most of your selfies,
there's some guy with a raised knife.

❖

You bought a suit made of
nicotine patches.

❖

Something's missing in your home,
and you desperately look for
someone to blame,
even though you live alone.

YOU MIGHT NEED A THERAPIST IF ...

After being diagnosed as bipolar,
you moved to Antarctica and
opened a gay bar.

❖

You're such a germaphobe, you sterilize
the sterilized gauze.

❖

A bum on the street asked if
you could spare a dime;
you gave him a quarter
and waited for change.

You named your kids after your favorite porn stars.

You are so skillful at blaming others,
politicians hire you
as a campaign consultant.

❖

Your PTSD is so bad, you hit the deck
when a sparrow farts.

❖

You spend Tuesdays cleaning
and sanitizing every inch of your
house, because Wednesdays
the maid comes.

You see *two* doors:
    #1 is "Stairway to Heaven"
    #2 is "Committee to Study
          How to Get to Heaven"
— you pick door #2.

❖

You date multiple-personality-disorder
women like Sybil so you can pretend
you're having an orgy.

❖

You're such a conversation hog,
even Jehovah's Witnesses no longer
come to your door.

Once a year you dress up like a woman
and wear makeup; and it so happens
you are a woman.

❖

You are very proud of your penis size
and measure it every day, at the mall.

❖

Your favorite practical joke is
to make a "Kick Me!" sign,
then tape it to your own back.

Whenever there's a crisis, anywhere in the world, you know it's your fault.

❖

You get homesick every time you drive by the state prison.

❖

You're such a stickler for detail, you wanted to be a Peeping Tom, but you couldn't do it because your name is Larry.

You're on a first name basis with
every pole dancer in the state.

❖

People think you're lonely because you
check your answering machine 10 times a
day; but you never listen to the messages,
you're calling just to hear your own voice.

❖

You suspect you might be a masochist
because you get upset when people don't
mistreat you right.

You're so indecisive, when filling out a
form, you can't get past "Mr.? or Ms.?"

❖

You're just sitting in the car, bored out of
your skull, but ain't nobody gonna
get *your* 15 minutes
left on the parking meter.

❖

Your mother only said "I love you" to
impress the neighbors.

YOU MIGHT NEED A THERAPIST IF ...

You're so cheap: you try to save money on acupunture
by sitting on a cactus.

YOU MIGHT NEED A THERAPIST IF ...

Your favorite pickup line is: "Hey babe, wanna help me use my condoms before their expiration date?"

❖

If the category existed, you could win the Nobel Prize for Bullshititure.

❖

Your wife says she wants to have sex in the backseat of a car, while you're driving.

You're such a perfectionist, the grass is
always greener on your side of the fence;
because you painted it,
one blade at a time.

❖

You have a different pair of underwear
for every day of the week,
but you only wear Monday's.

❖

You're so gutless, you keep trying to
commit suicide with an electric razor.

You'll lie even when the truth
sounds better.

❖

You're such a dyed-in-the-wool
Republican, you held the winning $100
million Powerball lottery ticket, but tore it
up rather than pay the taxes.

❖

You're such a dyed-in-the-wool Democrat,
you donated half of your $100 million
Powerball lottery winnings to charity
before the taxes were taken out.

YOU MIGHT NEED A THERAPIST IF ...

The prospect of kissing your sister
is wildly exciting, and so is
kissing your brother.

❖

You worry that your inferiority complex
is not as good as others.

❖

You're such a snob, your Shih Tzu's
doghouse has its own maid.

"You still live at home with your parents,
who still live at home with *their* parents!"

YOU MIGHT NEED A THERAPIST IF ...

You've been unemployed for three years,
but it's not the economy;
you can't find a listing in the
classified ads for "the boss".

❖

You consider traffic laws, speed limits,
and stop signs as merely a suggestion.

❖

You're so paranoid, you think
the voices in your head are
talking behind your back.

You plan your spontaneity.

❖

You tried to get in the
Guinness Book of World Records
by being the first to break all
Ten Commandments twice in one day.

❖

When it comes right down to it,
you'd sooner give up one of your
children than cigarettes.

Your home drug testing kits arrive by truck on a pallet.

❖

You're such an overachiever, the last time you donated blood you were upset because you couldn't give 100%.

❖

Whenever you go dancing, bystanders call 911 and report someone having an epileptic seizure.

You see yourself as a better person now that your spouse is on an antidepressant.

❖

You only play poker with mannequins so you can always win.

❖

You're so depressed, even the
You Might Need A Therapist If...
jokes fail to cheer you up.

When you withdraw money from
the bank, out of habit,
you always wear a ski mask.

❖

You think you have a stalker who
calls you three times a week,
but it's really the IRS.

❖

You're so overconfident, you put on a
condom before leaving the house
for a blind date.

You talk dirty to the clown
at fast food places.

❖

You have such a gambling addiction,
during the Super Bowl, after losing a $100
bet with a friend on a play, you made the
same bet on the instant replay.

❖

You get one hour's sleep each night
because that's how long it takes to
recharge your cell phone.

YOU MIGHT NEED A THERAPIST IF ...

You offer to rent one of your children
to a couple who can't conceive.

❖

You leave your husband for another man,
every two weeks or so.

❖

You think there are hidden messages
in your alphabet soup.

You wear your Halloween costume year round.

YOU MIGHT NEED A THERAPIST IF ...

The Adult Film industry has named you
an Honorary Patron of the Arts.

❖

Life gives you lemons, and you make
lemon *soup.*

❖

Your subtle way of flirting with men
is wearing see-through panties
to a singles' bar, and casually cleaning
your glasses with the hem of your dress.

YOU MIGHT NEED A THERAPIST IF ...

You're so bad at your job, you'd have
to suck to improve.

❖

Your motto is:
"The eyes are the window to...
my neighbor's bedroom."

❖

Sometimes you won't eat anything all day
unless it's a free sample.

You started at an entry level position
and over the next 20 years put your
heart and soul into working your way
to the top with one objective in mind:
So you could fire people.

❖

Your marriage proposal was: "Are you
tired of masturbating yet?"

❖

You unwaveringly live your life
to the letter of the law;
unfortunately it's Murphy's.

You lick the same postage stamp
for more than 5 minutes.

YOU MIGHT NEED A THERAPIST IF ...

You don't give a damn about what the future holds in store; you only go to fortune tellers to argue with them.

❖

For the past year you've double checked your losing lottery ticket every day, just in case.

❖

You've gone bankrupt from attending all those "Wealth & Abundance" seminars.

YOU MIGHT NEED A THERAPIST IF ...

You have to divorce someone in order to really get to know them.

❖

You locked your dog and your girlfriend in the garage for 12 hours to find out which one would be happiest to see you.

❖

To make sure you get your monies worth, you eat a bag of Oreo Cookies right before having your teeth cleaned.

YOU MIGHT NEED A THERAPIST IF ...

You carry duct tape, rope, and a shovel
in the trunk of your car.

❖

You wear your pajamas to the airport and
dress after the security check.

❖

You're so dishonest you give politics
a good name.

YOU MIGHT NEED A THERAPIST IF ...

When the drunk guy you just met
in a bar brags he got off scot-free
after killing his wife, you smile and
coyly reply, "So... you're single then?"

❖

You read the commandment,
"Love Thy Neighbor",
then went out and bought condoms.

❖

You ran out of bar soap six months ago
and still haven't noticed.

For Lent you give up celibacy.

❖

When you get a sundae to go,
you make them put the cherry
in a separate container.

❖

Your closet consists entirely of
camouflage outfits.

YOU MIGHT NEED A THERAPIST IF ...

You ordered custom printed toilet paper
with your ex-wife's picture on each sheet.

❖

You masturbate to *Field & Stream*.

❖

Your idea of a vacation is to go
to a different bar.

YOU MIGHT NEED A THERAPIST IF ...

You were a prostitute for six months
and never sold anything.

❖

You are such a player, you go to work
every day from a different direction.

❖

You steal fish from the supermarket and
eat it while you're still shopping.

YOU MIGHT NEED A THERAPIST IF ...

Your excuse for talking to yourself is:
"There's no one else I can trust."

❖

You and your wife are drowning
and you try to save the boat anchor
because it was very expensive.

❖

You break into tears when you see
Battered Shrimp on the menu.

You're an incurable kleptomaniac,
but you only steal clothes that are
on sale, figuring if you get caught
you can argue for a reduced sentence.

❖

Your expectations are so low,
your ideal date is:
"Someone who doesn't fall face down
drunk in his spaghetti."

❖

You're so overprotective of your kid, you
installed a seatbelt on his skateboard.

The TV show *Hoarders*
won't stop calling you.

❖

You sleep in every day,
but it's not your house.

❖

You joined the NRA even though
the most powerful weapon you own
is a squirt gun.

You're such a compulsive eater,
your dream house has two kitchens.

❖

Every year your family vacations
at Betty Ford.

❖

You get depressed when things are
going well and you can't think of
anything to worry about.

You're such an egomaniac you think
you're overqualified to play God.

❖

You can only enjoy sex while
watching *Family Feud.*

❖

You have reverse-paranoia:
When you walk down a busy street,
you fear you're following someone.

*You're so miserly; you use old shoelaces
for dental floss.*

What others call "multiple personalities"
you call "multi-talented".

❖

You only speak English, but you can curse
fluently in ten different languages.

❖

Your method for getting rid of a
bad mood is to pass it on.

You're such a narcissist, you can't look in a mirror without getting an erection.

❖

Your lips say no, but your hips say yes.

❖

Your motto is:
"If you can't beat 'em... shoot 'em."

You know meditation would
probably help, if you could only
sit still long enough.

❖

You never forget an offense; you even
tracked down the doctor who slapped
your rear at birth, and beat him up.

❖

You never put off until tomorrow what you
can con someone else into doing today.

You are now self-employed and you still
have a boss who's an asshole.

❖

You fake an orgasm even
when you masturbate.

❖

It's not your imagination —
everyone IS out to get you.

YOU MIGHT NEED A THERAPIST IF ...

You feel inferior because your inner child
is taller than you.

❖

You love your wife so much,
you almost told her.

❖

You're so vain, you probably think
these jokes are about you.

THE AUTHORS

Comedian **John Carfi** often appears on television. He also performs his unique style of humor, headlining in world famous comedy clubs, casinos, theaters, concert halls, cruise ships, corporate shows and just about every venue known to mankind. He hosted his own morning radio shows on Rock and Country stations WZZO, WPMR and WDLS. He performs in front of thousands of people each week nationwide, and opens in concert with many superstars. He and Cliff are the co-authors of ten comedy books including two best sellers; and he's written jokes for comedians such as Joan Rivers. For more info: **www.johncarfi.com**

Writer and editor, **Cliff Carle,** used to perform stand-up comedy at The Improv and The Comedy Store. He also wrote material for other comedians, including Joan Rivers. In 1983, Cliff and John founded CCC Publications, a publishing company that released 200 titles and launched the careers of many humor writers. Cliff currently owns an editorial and publishing consultant business. For more info: **www.cliffcarle.com**

Co-writer **David W. Earle, LPC** is a mental health counselor helping clients with anger management, substance abuse, compulsive gambling, eating disorders, anxiety, depression, and relationships. He holds a Master's of Science from Texas A&M. David combines healing arts with twenty-plus years of executive management to teach leadership skills. He is also a trainer, coach, alternative dispute professional, and author of numerous self-help books. For more info google: **Psychology Today – David W. Earle, LPC**

THE ILLLUSTRATOR

Scott Sackett has been drawing cartoons all his life. In grammar school he drew tiny figures in the margins of his homework, distracting him from getting any decent grades. In high school, he was the staff cartoonist on the school newspaper subjecting his fellow students to an army of inventive characters, and his teachers and the faculty to witty, and sometimes scathing caricatures—no one was safe.

Scott attended Columbia College in Chicago, and later Sheridan College in Ontario, Canada, where he combined his two passions, drawing funny pictures and making home movies. He graduated with a BA in Film and a degree in Character Animation.

Upon moving to Los Angeles he became a storyboard artist for Animation Television Production. He also freelances, illustrating books and cartoons for clients. This is his fourth such book.

If you have a project on the burner and need designs, illustrations, cartoons, or caricatures, please visit:
www.scottcackettla.com

NEWEST BOOKS by JOHN CARFI & CLIFF CARLE

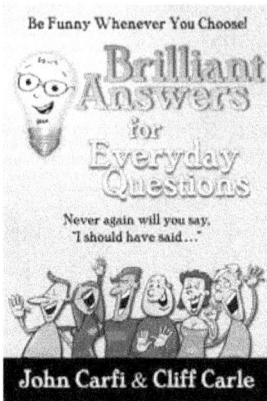

BRILLIANT ANSWERS FOR EVERYDAY
QUESTIONS
(e-book)

How would you like to be the person everyone is waiting for...to arrive at the party, the office, the restaurant, or wherever? What if, in a very short amount of time, you could develop a reputation for being a funny guy or gal? With BRILLIANT ANSWERS it will be quick, easy, and fun. Never again will you be at a loss for funny or clever words. Almost daily you are bombarded with annoying questions; and you probably answer 90% of them seriously, and 10% jokingly. Imagine if you flipped those percentages around? People would then start to see you differently. And when they are putting together a guest list for their next party, or get-together, guess who's going to be in the number one slot: clever YOU! (aka The Fun Guy! / The Fun Gal!)

KILLER VOICEMAIL
(e-book)

Voicemail is no longer just a means of identifying yourself and prompting a response, it's now an entertainment medium. Express your inner comic and treat your callers to loads of laughs with over 130 funny and clever outgoing messages for your cell phone or answering service. For ease of use and to find the perfect message for you, the book is divided into nine categorical chapters. Amuse your friends when they call and you're not available—or just not in the mood to talk. Have fun and spread the laughter!

GLEE-MAIL
(e-book)

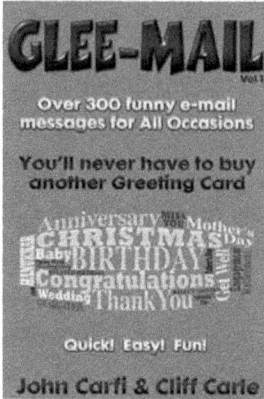

This book is useful year-round since occasions for greetings never end. Who isn't obliged to acknowledge friends and relatives? And GLEE-MAIL makes it 10 times easier than driving to the drug store, walking the greeting card aisles, picking a card, putting it back, picking another card, putting it back until you find the right (overpriced at $6.95) one. Then standing in line to buy it and drive back home—only to realize you should've picked that other card you passed on! With GLEE-MAIL you simply go to the appropriate chapter, scan the e-greetings, pick one you like, then type and hit SEND. Just think about it: you're getting over 300 funny e-mailable messages for less than the price of ONE greeting card!

SAMPLE E-GREETING:
Here's wishing you a Merry Christmas and a Happy New Year!
And if you're Jewish: Happy Hanukkah!
And if you're Atheist: Happy Nothingness!

BOOKS BY DAVID W. EARLE

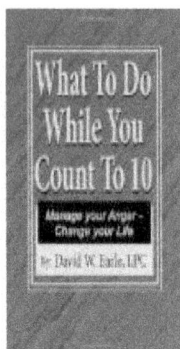

Can anger be positive? Using anger correctly usually has positive results! As difficult as this concept seems to most people it is true. *What To Do While You Count To 10* teaches effective emotional management required for a successful relationship; one that yields love instead of destruction.

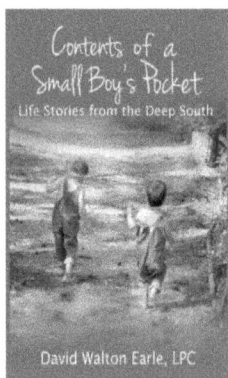

Any mother who ever raised a small boy learns to check his pockets before she washes his well-patched blue jeans for his various valuables and surprises. *Contents of a Small Boy's Pocket* is everyday life and promises to make you laugh, cry, be angry, and challenged with some life's uncertainty but most of all, you will enjoy the read.

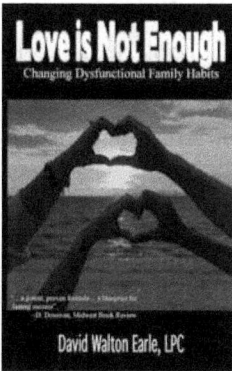

Love is Not Enough explains seven destructive habits and provides antidotes for each so you can fully express yourself with the love you truly wanted to give, what your family wants to receive, and what they deserve. Until you *unlearn* your learned dysfunctional habit, love will never *be enough.*

Communication is the key to any successful relationship, business, or venture. Improve your current communication skills and increase the love you receive, enhance the love you wish to extend, improve your productivity, and give happiness a better chance for success.

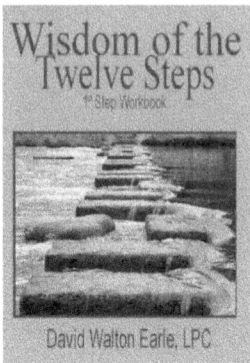

Wisdom of the Twelve Steps
1st Step Workbook

David Walton Earle, LPC

This volume of the *Wisdom of the Twelve Steps* is one book in a series specifically written to assist the recovering community on their journey toward peace and serenity. This workbook helps those who suffer from compulsive gambling, sex addiction, eating disorders, compulsive shopping, drug / alcohol addictions, internet / electronic obsession, etc., and anyone who loves someone with any of these debilitating problems. Use this book as a visual and tangible guide on your miraculous journey.

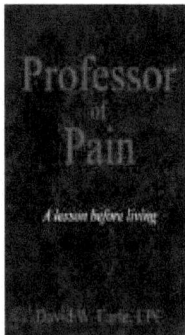

Professor of Pain
A lesson before living

David W. Earle, LPC

The *Professor of Pain* teaches the lessons for successful and happy lives; it takes the reader on the author's painful journey learning these necessary lessons. This book uses a unique hybrid combination of poetry and narrative to weave a tapestry of new understanding and awareness.

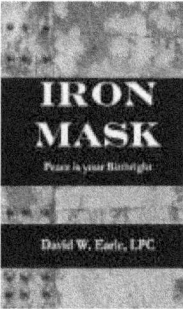

Share life's lessons, gained from painful experiences; celebrate triumph over adversity. *If chaos is your companion, where have you hidden your peace?*

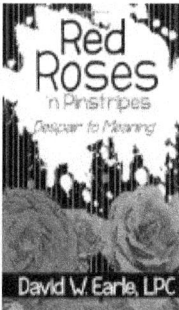

Red Roses 'n Pinstripes is torrid romance together with the ravages of war and its deadly companion, death and dedicated to all those who loved and lost. So here's to those who enter love's classroom - learn from each experience and continue to love and still smile.

FAMOUS BLURBS

Dead or alive, YOU MIGHT NEED A THERAPIST IF will have you laughing historically...

Funniest book I ever read! And you know me,
I cannot tell a lie!
— GEORGE WASHINGTON

I laughed my head off!
— MARIE ANTOINETTE

Me too!
— ICHABOD CRANE

Buying this book was the smartest thing I ever did!
— ALBERT EINSTEIN

I had an axe to grind until I read this book!
— LIZZIE BORDEN

Da jokes come atcha like a machine gun. I love deese wiseguys. Youse kill me!
— AL CAPONE

I keep this book inside my jacket next to my heart at all times and frequently check to make sure it's still there!

— NAPOLEON BONAPARTE

Woe is me! My signed copy is missing and I'm still looking for it!

— AMELIA EARHART

Shucks, this book is OK by me!

— WYATT EARP

With each joke a lightbulb goes on in my head:
Why didn't I think of that one!?

— THOMAS EDISON

You guys drive me nuts! All new stuff!
No assembly-line humor here!

— HENRY FORD

The jokes hit you like a bolt of lightning!

— BENJAMIN FRANKLIN

I never dreamed I'd like jokes that were so complex!
— SIGMUND FREUD

I loved it and I hated it!
— DR. JEKYLL AND MR. HYDE

These jokes left me with a burning desire for more!
— JOAN OF ARC

I never laugh, but this book made me surrender to the urge!
— ROBERT E. LEE

Ask not what a joke can do for you,
ask where you can buy this book!
— JOHN F. KENNEDY

So funny I read it four score and seven times!
— "HONEST ABE" LINCOLN

Wish I had printed this book!
— JOHANNES GUTENBERG

Gentlemen, your sex jokes got me so hot, I thought I'd cry!
— MARILYN MONROE

I had a dream that someday there'd be a book this funny!
— MARTIN LUTHER KING JR.

You don't have to get hit in the head to appreciate the gravity of these jokes!

— SIR ISAAC NEWTON

These writers have a real sick sense of humor!

— FLORENCE NIGHTINGALE

I heard about THERAPIST IF in the middle of the night and couldn't wait for the bookstore to open, so I broke in and burglarized my copy!

— RICHARD NIXON

*When the team is up against it, and the breaks
are beating the boys,
I read a joke for the Gipper!*

— KNUTE ROCKNE

The date this book was published shall live in infamy!

— FRANKLIN D. ROOSEVELT

Dudes, you really knocked one out of the ballpark!

— BABE RUTH

To be, or not to be laughing? THERAPIST IF answers the question!

— WILLIAM SHAKESPEARE

I drink to your success!

— SOCRATES

You guys' sense of humor is unreal!

— SANTA CLAUS, EASTER BUNNY & TOOTH FAIRY

*I'd buy this book again even if the only place it's on sale
is a leper colony!*

— MOTHER TERESA

*My deepest thanks to the archaeologists for
digging me up in time to read this book.
I've been wrapped up in it ever since!*

— TUTANKHAMUN

*Finally it's here! I've been keeping an ear out
for word of your funny book!*

— VINCENT VAN GOGH

Who needs food when you've got jokes
like these to sustain you!?

— MAHATMA GANDI

I was misquoted! As I rode from town to town I was yelling,
"THERAPIST IF is coming! THERAPIST IF is coming!"

— PAUL REVERE

Every joke hits a bull's-eye!

— ANNIE OAKLEY

There are not enough words to express
my appreciation of your humor!

— NOAH WEBSTER